75 Homemade Macaroni Salad Recipes

(75 Homemade Macaroni Salad Recipes - Volume 1)

Elise Tobin

Content

75 Awesome Macaroni Salad Recipes

***

1. Apricot Macaroni Salad Recipe

Serving: 8 | Prep: | Cook: 60mins | Ready in:

Ingredients

- 8 oz macaroni: cooked and drained
- 20, oz pineapple chunks, drained
- 1/2 cup chopped red or green or combos of both bell peppers
- 1/2 cup shredded cheddar cheese
- 2/3 cup mayonaisse
- 1/2 cup apricot preserves
- salt and pepper to taste

Direction

- Combine mayo and apricot preserves.
- Mix all other ingredients together and then blend in apricot mayo.
- Season to taste.
- Chill 1 hour before serving.

2. Aunt Bonnies Ring Macaroni Tuna Salad Recipe

Serving: 8 | Prep: | Cook: 15mins | Ready in:

Ingredients

- 1 (7 ounce) box ring macaroni, prepared as directed on box
- 1 (8 1/2 ounce) can Le Sueur early june peas, drained (or 1 cup Green Giant Select Le Sueur frozen baby peas, thawed)
- 1 cup celery, finely diced
- 2 (6 ounce) cans tuna, drained
- 1/4 cup onions, finely diced
- 1 cup Miracle Whip
- 1 teaspoon salt (or less, use to taste)

Direction

- Gently mix all ingredients together and refrigerate 2 to 3 hours.

3. Awsome Macaroni Salad Recipe

Serving: 6 | Prep: | Cook: 11mins | Ready in:

Ingredients

- 1 16oz bag of elbow macaroni
- 1 small green bellpepper, diced small
- 1 small red bellpepper, diced small
- 2 celery ribs, thinly sliced
- 1 cup mayo
- 1 squirt ketchup (optional)
- 1 small package of frozen cooked shrimp, thawed (optional)
- salt to taste

Direction

- Boil Pasta according to package directions
- Add rest of ingredients, except shrimp, mayo and ketchup mix well
- Mix mayo and ketchup add to rest of ingredients and mix thoroughly
- Add shrimp and make sure all ingredients are coated with mayo
- Chill in refrigerator
- Enjoy!!

4. BBQ Macaroni Salad Recipe

Serving: 10 | Prep: | Cook: 12mins | Ready in:

Ingredients

- Most recipes for barbecue-flavored macaroni salad drown the pasta in ketchupy barbecue sauce, creating a salad that is much too sweet and sticky. Here's what we discovered about how to produce a well-balanced smoky and spicy side dish.
- Test Kitchen Discoveries
- A combination of mayonnaise and barbecue sauce is more effective than barbecue sauce alone, as the tang of the barbecue sauce is balanced by the neutral creaminess of the mayonnaise.
- This salad works best with a sweet, smoky-flavored barbecue sauce.
- If the salad sits and becomes dry, adding a little warm water will make it creamy again.
- table salt
- 1 pound elbow macaroni
- 1 red bell pepper , seeded and chopped fine
- 1 rib celery , chopped fine
- 4 scallions , sliced thin
- 2 tablespoons cider vinegar
- 1 teaspoon hot sauce
- 1 teaspoon chili powder
- 1/8 teaspoon garlic powder
- Pinch cayenne pepper
- 1 cup mayonnaise
- 1/2 cup barbecue sauce (see note above)
- ground black pepper

Direction

- 1. Bring 4 quarts water to boil in large pot. Add 1 tablespoon salt and macaroni and cook until nearly tender, about 5 minutes. Drain in colander and rinse with cold water until cool, then drain once more, briefly, so that pasta is still moist; transfer to large bowl.
- 2. Stir in bell pepper, celery, scallions, vinegar, hot sauce, chili powder, garlic powder, and cayenne pepper, and let sit until flavors are absorbed, about 2 minutes. Stir in mayonnaise and barbecue sauce and let sit until salad is no longer watery, about 5 minutes. Season with salt and pepper and serve. (The salad can be covered and refrigerated for up to 2 days. Check seasonings before serving.)

5. BLT MACARONI SALAD Recipe

Serving: 6 | Prep: | Cook: | Ready in:

Ingredients

- 1 box elbow macaroni (8oz)
- 2/3 cup mayonaise
- 1/3 cup plain yogurt
- 1 tbsp vinegar
- 1/4 tsp each salt & pepper
- 8 slices bacon; cooked & crumbled
- 3 green onions finely chopped
- 1 large tomato chopped
- Chopped romaine lettuce (bitesize pieces)

Direction

- Cook pasta according to package directions.
- Drain and rinse.
- Set aside.
- Meanwhile in a large bowl, combine mayo, yogurt, vinegar, salt and pepper.
- Add pasta and remaining ingredients to mayo mixture.
- Cover and refrigerate until ready to serve.
- Up to 24 hours. (After the 24 hour mark the lettuce sogs)

6. BLT Macaroni Salad Recipe

Serving: 6 | Prep: | Cook: 30mins | Ready in:

Ingredients

- 1/2 cup mayonnaise
- 3 tablespoons chili sauce
- 2 tablespoons lemon juice
- 1 teaspoon sugar
- 3 cups cooked elbow macaroni
- 1/2 cup chopped seeded tomato
- 2 tablespoons chopped green onions
- 3 cups shredded lettuce
- 4 bacon strips, cooked and crumbled

Direction

- In a large bowl, combine the first four ingredients. Add the macaroni, tomatoes and onions; toss to coat. Cover and refrigerate. Just before serving, add lettuce and bacon; toss to coat. Yield: 6 servings.
- Comments
- Re: BLT Macaroni Salad
- Excellent salad just made it and had to give it a taste. Give it a 10.
- Didn't have any chili sauce so just added a bit of chili powder...Also added a bit more bacon, never can have too much bacon.

7. Bacon Tomato Pasta Macaroni Salad Recipe

Serving: 8 | Prep: | Cook: 10mins | Ready in:

Ingredients

- 2 cups uncooked elbow macaroni
- 5 green onions finely chopped
- 2 large tomatoes diced
- 1-1/4 cup celery diced
- 1-1/4 cup mayonnaise
- 5 teaspoons white vinegar
- 1/4 teaspoon salt
- 1/4 teaspoon pepper
- 1 pound cooked bacon crumbled

Direction

- Cook macaroni according to package directions then drain and rinse in cold water.
- In large bowl combine macaroni, green onions, tomatoes and celery.
- Combine mayonnaise, vinegar, salt and pepper then pour over macaroni mixture.
- Stir to coat and put in rectangular baking pan then cover and chill for 2 hours.
- Just before serving add bacon.

8. Bills Simple Macaroni Salad But Simply Delicious Recipe

Serving: 16 | Prep: | Cook: 10mins | Ready in:

Ingredients

- 1 (16 ounce) package macaroni
- 8 ea hard boiled eggs, chopped; or more or none
- 2 red bell peppers, chopped
- 1 green bell pepper, chopped; optional
- 1 bunch chopped green onions
- 1 ea onion, medium; diced
- 5 stalk celery, diced (optional); or more
- 1 ea parsley, 1/4 bunch; cut finely
- 1 tablespoon olive oil
- 1 cup mayonnaise
- 1 cup buttermilk
- 4 tbsp vinegar
- 1 packet dry vegetable soup mix or more; onion soup optional
- shrimp for decoration with paprika
- 1/4 cup relish
- 4 ea parsley stems with leaves
- 1/2 cup pickle juice
- 1 tbsp. mustard djion type wet
- 1 tablespoon celery salt
- 1 tablespoon poatato salad seasoning salt

Direction

- Bring a large pot of lightly salted water to a boil with uncooked eggs in it. Add pasta and cook for 8 to 10 minutes, or until al dente. Drain, and rinse with cold water until no longer hot. Transfer noodles to a large bowl.

- Cool, peel and chop eggs and mix in chopped eggs with noodles.
- Stir in red bell peppers, green bell peppers, green onions, onion, celery and olive oil. Mix in mayonnaise, vinegar and soup mix and rest of ingredients except shrimp and eggs. Refrigerate at least a few hours before serving. I wait overnight and add more buttermilk if dry.
- Before decorating, check to see if pasta has absorbed all the liquid and add more buttermilk, if necessary. Decorate with shrimp and paprika or Old Bay before serving.

9. Birthday Pasta Salad Recipe

Serving: 0 | Prep: | Cook: 30mins | Ready in:

Ingredients

- 1 lb. salad macaroni (ditalini)
- 1 cup Vegenaise or regular mayonnaise
- 2 tsp yellow mustard
- 1 tbls white vinegar
- 1 tbls parsley
- 2 tsp granulated onion
- 2 cloves of garlic, minced
- 1 medium red onion, diced
- 3-4 stalks of celery, diced
- 2 cucumbers, diced
- 2 cups small cherry tomatoes
- 1 cup black olives, sliced
- 1 cans of garbanzo beans, well rinsed
- salt and pepper to taste

Direction

- Put water on to boil. Clean and chop veggies. Rinse beans. Boil pasta until al dente. Drain and rinse with cold water until pasta is cool to the touch. Mix in mayo, mustard, spices, veggies, and beans. Salt and pepper to taste.

Place in fridge for at least 4 hours; overnight is best. Taste again before serving and if necessary add additional salt, pepper, mustard, granulated onion or granulated garlic.

10. Black Eyed Pea And Macaroni Salad Recipe

Serving: 4 | Prep: | Cook: | Ready in:

Ingredients

- 1/2 cup cold black-eyed peas
- 1 pound package elbow macaroni cooked and cooled
- 2 tablespoons sweet pickle relish
- 1/4 cup mayonnaise
- 1/4 cup chopped green bell peppers
- 1/4 cup chopped celery

Direction

- Mix and serve on lettuce leaves.

11. Blt Macaroni Salad Recipe

Serving: 0 | Prep: | Cook: 30mins | Ready in:

Ingredients

- BLT macaroni Salad -
- 1/2 cup mayonnaise
- 3 tablespoons chili sauce
- 2 tablespoons lemon juice
- 1 teaspoon sugar
- 3 cups elbow macaroni, cooked
- 1/2 cup tomato, seeded and chopped
- 2 tablespoons green onions, chopped
- 3 cups lettuce, shredded 4 slices cooked bacon, crumbled
- thx to:

- Berty Scialla-vazquez shared Lauren Weido's photo.

Direction

- Directions:
- 1. In a large bowl, combine the first four ingredients; mix well.
- 2. Add the macaroni, tomato and onions; toss to coat.
- 3. Cover and refrigerate.
- 4. Just before serving, add lettuce and bacon; toss to coat

12. Blue Cheese Macaroni Salad Recipe

Serving: 8 | Prep: | Cook: 10mins | Ready in:

Ingredients

- blue cheese macaroni Salad
- 4 ounces elbow macaroni
- 1/2 cup coarsely chopped walnuts
- 1/2 cup reduced-fat mayonnaise
- 1 1/2 teaspoon dijon-style mustard
- 1-2 ounces blue cheese, crumbled
- 1/2 cup halved seedless grapes

Direction

- Cook macaroni according to package directions; drain and set aside to cool.
- Mix together walnuts, mayonnaise, mustard, blue cheese and grape halves. Combine with cooled pasta and refrigerate until ready to serve.

13. CHICKEN MACARONI SALAD Recipe

Serving: 10 | Prep: | Cook: 30mins | Ready in:

Ingredients

- 1/2 KG OF macaroni pasta
- 1/2 KG OF chicken MEAT
- 1 MEDIUM SIZE CAN OF pineapple tidbits (450 grms)
- 50 grms of raisins
- 500 grms to 1 kg of mayonaise (ITS UP TO YOU)
- 100 grms of kraft cheese
- 1 piece of carrots
- 1 onion
- salt AND pepper TO TASTE
- 1/4 can of condense milk (about 125 grms)
- a spoonfull of sweet pickle relish

Direction

- Bring to a boil with salt the macaroni pasta, drain and set aside
- Bring to a boil the chicken meat with salt, drain and set aside
- Drain pineapple tidbits
- Cut into cubes the cheese, carrot and onion
- Cut into small cubes or thinly the chicken meat
- Get a big bowl and begin to mix all the ingredients carefully one by one. First put in the bowl the pasta then the chicken, pineapple tidbits, raisins, cheese, carrots, onion, sweet pickle relish, condense milk and mayonnaise. Salt and pepper to taste. Mix well but carefully. Adding more mayonnaise is depends of your taste. Put on the salad rack and chill for at least an hour before you eat. So try and enjoy this simple CHICKEN MACARONI SALAD. IT'S SO DELICIOUS.

14. Cajun Macaroni Salad Recipe

Serving: 10 | Prep: | Cook: 40mins | Ready in:

Ingredients

- 2 lbs shrimp, unpeeled with heads on
- 1 quart water

- 2 tbs liquid crab boil
- 1 medium onion, quartered
- 3 tbs salt
- 1 1/2 cups uncooked elbow macaroni
- 1 large onion, chopped
- 1 cup chopped celery
- 1/2 lb bacon, cooked, drained and crushed. Reserve bacon fat.
- 1 tbs garlic, minced
- 1 cup fresh parsley chopped
- 5 boiled egges
- 1 tsp cayenne pepper
- 1 tsp salt
- 1 tsp crab boil
- 1 cup mayonnaise
- reserved bacon fat
- 1 tbs paprika

Direction

- Cook shrimp with heads on and unpeeled in 1 quart of water. Add 2 tbsp. of crab boil and medium quartered onion to water and boil for 20 minutes.
- Remove from heat and add 3 tbsp. of salt, stir and let stand for 5 minutes. Drain and peel shrimp. Reserve liquid and cook the elbow macaroni in it until al dente.
- In a large bowl, combine drained macaroni, chopped onion, celery, bacon, garlic, chopped egg whites and parsley.
- In a separate bowl, combine mashed egg yellows with 1 tsp. salt, 1 tsp. cayenne, 1 tsp. crab boil, mayonnaise and bacon fat until well blended.
- Add to macaroni and mix well. Sprinkle paprika on top.

15. Cheddar Macaroni Salad Recipe

Serving: 4 | Prep: | Cook: 10mins | Ready in:

Ingredients

- 1 cup elbow or medium shell macaroni

- 3/4 cup cubed cheddar cheese
- 1 stalk celery sliced
- 1/2 small green bell pepper chopped
- 1/2 cup frozen peas thawed
- 1/3 cup chopped onion
- 1/4 cup mayonnaise
- 1/4 cup sour cream
- 2 tablespoons milk
- 2 tablespoons sweet pickle relish

Direction

- Cook macaroni according to package directions then drain and rinse with cold water.
- Drain again.
- Combine macaroni, cheese, celery, bell pepper, peas and onion then stir gently to combine.
- Mix mayonnaise, sour cream, milk, pickle relish, and 1/4 teaspoon salt then toss with macaroni.
- Cover and chill several hours or overnight then stir in additional milk if necessary.

16. Cheese And Macaroni Salad Recipe

Serving: 6 | Prep: | Cook: 15mins | Ready in:

Ingredients

- 2 cups uncooked elbow macaroni
- 10 ounces frozen sweet peas
- 2 cups shredded cheddar cheese
- 4 green onions, sliced, about 1/2 cup
- 1/2 cup sliced celery
- 1 cup mayonnaise
- 1/3 cup sweet pickle relish
- 1/2 teaspoon salt
- 1 head iceberg lettuce, turn into bite-sized pieces, about 3 cups
- 1/2 cup bacon crumbles

Direction

- Cook macaroni according to package directions.
- Rinse frozen peas under running water to separate.
- Mix macaroni, peas, cheese, onions, celery, mayonnaise, relish and salt.
- Cover and refrigerate for 1 hour.
- Just before serving, toss with lettuce and bacon crumbles.
- Cheese and bologna salad:
- Substitute 1 cup cut-up bacon for the bacon crumbles.
- Cheese and chicken salad:
- Substitute 1 cup cooked chicken or turkey for the cheese.
- Cheese and frank salad;
- Substitute 3 hot dogs, cooked and sliced, for the bacon.
- Cheese and shrimp salad:
- Substitute 6 ounces of shrimp for the cheese.

17. Cheezy Mac Salad Recipe

Serving: 6 | Prep: | Cook: 20mins | Ready in:

Ingredients

- 1 pkg mac and cheeze (powered cheeze)
- 1/2 cup mayo
- chopped onions, peppers mushrooms, diced ham etc

Direction

- Cook the mac according to directions
- Mix the mayo and cheese powder together
- Mix the mac, and dressing together, and throw in the other stuff to taste

18. Chicken Macaroni Salad Filipino Style Recipe

Serving: 8 | Prep: | Cook: 30mins | Ready in:

Ingredients

- 1 box macaroni noodles
- 2-3 big chicken breast
- mayonnaise
- 1 can pineapple chunks or tidbits
- 1 onion
- 1/2 cup sweet pickle relish
- 1 cup shredded cheddar cheese
- 1/2 cup raisins
- 2 to 3 medium sized carrots(optional)
- salt
- pepper

Direction

- Boil chicken breast in water with salt and pepper until it's tender. Drain chicken and shred it in 1 inch length.
- Peal skin and boil carrots in water for 15-20 minutes or until cooked. Drain carrots and let it cool. (OPTIONAL)
- Cook macaroni noodles according to package cooking instructions. Make sure it's el dente. Drain and cool.
- Drain pineapple chunks or tidbits.
- Finely chop onions
- Combine the macaroni, shredded chicken, pineapple, sweet pickle relish, raisins, shredded cheese, carrots, and slowly add the mayonnaise while mixing all ingredients. (You can put more or less mayo in your salad, all up to you)
- Add salt and pepper to taste.
- Refrigerate, then serve.

19. Chicken Macaroni Salad Recipe

Serving: 8 | Prep: | Cook: 60mins | Ready in:

Ingredients

- 500 grams elbow macaroni
- 1 large chicken breast, boiled and shredded
- 1 cup boiled, diced carrots
- 1 cup raisins
- 1 cup diced sweet ham
- 1 cup frozen peas
- 1 cup pineapple chunks
- 1/2 cup diced red capsicum
- 3 cups mayonnaise or any low-cal equivalent (adjust to suit taste)
- dash of salt and pepper

Direction

- Boil macaroni according to package instructions. Drain and set aside.
- In a large bowl, mix all the ingredients then season to taste.
- Chill for at least 1 hour before serving.

20. Classic Macaroni Salad Recipe

Serving: 8 | Prep: | Cook: 2hours | Ready in:

Ingredients

- 2 cups dry macaroni
- 1 cup sliced celery
- 1 cup chopped green pepper (or half red and half green)
- 1/4 cup minced onion
- 2/3 cup mayonnaise
- 1 tablespoon yellow mustard
- 2 teaspoons sugar
- 1/2 teaspoon salt
- 1/8 teaspoon black pepper

Direction

- Begin by preparing the macaroni according to package directions. Do not add any salt. When the macaroni is tender rinse it in cool water and drain well. Next chop and measure the vegetables. Meanwhile, in a large bowl

combine all of the other ingredients. This is the dressing. Mix it well. Add the prepared macaroni and vegetables. Mix well and chill for 2 hours, or until serving time.
- *Add whatever you like. Olives, chopped cooked egg, dill, cheese, parsley, etc... (But I prefer it just the way it is)

21. Cool And Creamy Macaroni Salad Recipe

Serving: 10 | Prep: | Cook: 25mins | Ready in:

Ingredients

- salt
- 1lb elbow macaroni
- 1/2 small red onion,minced
- 1 celery rib,minced
- 1/2c minced fresh parsley leaves
- 2 tbs. juice from 1 lemon
- 1Tbs Dijon mustard
- 1/8tsp garlic powder
- pinch of cayenne
- 11/2c mayonnaise
- ground black pepper

Direction

- Bring 4qts. water to boil in large pot. Add 1Tbs salt and macaroni and cook till just nearly tender, about 5 mins. Drain and rinse with cold water till cool, then drain briefly so macaroni remains moist. Transfer to large bowl.
- Stir in onion, celery, parsley, lemon juice, mustard, garlic powder, and cayenne and let sit until flavors are absorbed, about 2 mins. Add mayonnaise and let sit until salad texture is no longer watery, 5 to 10 mins. Season with salt and pepper to taste.
- Can be made up to 2 days ahead. Stir in a little warm water to loosen texture, if necessary.

22. Cool And Creamy Macaroni Salad W/roasted Peppers Recipe

Serving: 8 | Prep: | Cook: 25mins | Ready in:

Ingredients

- salt and pepper
- 1 pound elbow macaroni
- 1/4 cup minced red onion or use regular yellow onion
- 1 celery rib, minced
- 1/4 cup finely chopped parsley
- 2 T. lemon juice
- 1 T. Dijon mustard (heaping Tablespoon)
- 1/2 t. garlic powder
- 1/2 t. cayenne pepper
- 1 cup drained jarred roasted red peppers, chopped
- 1 1/2 cups mayonnaise (see brief intro)

Direction

- Cook pasta. Bring 4 quarts water to boil in large pot. Add 1 tablespoon salt and pasta and cook until al dente, 6 to 8 minutes. Drain in colander and rinse with cold water until cool. Drain again briefly and transfer to large bowl.
- MAKE DRESSING: Stir in onion, celery, parsley, lemon juice, mustard, garlic powder, cayenne, and roasted red peppers. Add mayonnaise and let sit until salad is no longer watery, 5 to 10 minutes. Season with salt and pepper. Serve. (Salad can be refrigerated, covered, for about 2 days.)

23. Creole Macaroni Salad Recipe

Serving: 6 | Prep: | Cook: 15mins | Ready in:

Ingredients

- 4 cups cooked macaroni (6 or 7 ounces or 2 cups uncooked)
- 2 cups diced tomatoes
- 1 cup grated sharp cheddar cheese, or your favorite!
- 1 cup mayonnaise
- 1/4 cup sliced pimiento stuffed olives
- 1/2 small onion, grated
- 1 - 2 cloves garlic, more or less, depending on your taste
- 1/8 teaspoon cayenne pepper, or more if you like

Direction

- If macaroni is uncooked, prepare according to package directions, boiling until tender, but not mushy, blanch (rinse well in cold water), drain until thoroughly dry.
- Mix all together.
- Refrigerate several hours (at least 4), or overnight.
- Can be served on lettuce leaves or just as it is.
- Enjoy!

24. Deli Style Mac Salad Recipe

Serving: 10 | Prep: | Cook: 40mins | Ready in:

Ingredients

- I box of macaroni, various shapes and sizes
- 4-5 carrots finely chopped
- 3 celery stalks
- Half of a red onion
- 3/4 cup mayonnaise
- Dash of garlic powder, dash of celery salt, black pepper
- Baby tomatoes

Direction

- Boil macaroni as directed, drain. Throw finely chopped veggies in big bowl with macaroni, stir in mayo, and seasonings, garnish with baby tomatoes halved. Serve chilled.

25. Easy Macaroni Salad Recipe

Serving: 10 | Prep: | Cook: 10mins | Ready in:

Ingredients

- 3 cups elbow macaroni
- 1/2 cup mayonaise
- 1/2 cup lemon poppyseed salad dressing
- 1 carrot
- 1 red pepper
- 2 green onions
- 1/2 green olive slices
- 1 can corn
- 1 can chicken

Direction

- Cook the macaroni in a large pot of boiling salted water, drain and rinse with cold water until it is cool
- Peel and dice the carrot
- Seed and dice the red pepper
- Finely slice the onion
- Drain the corn, chicken, and olives
- Combine all ingredients in a large bowl
- It tastes better if it has a couple hours in the fridge for the flavours to mix.

26. Easy Pasta Salad Recipe

Serving: 0 | Prep: | Cook: 20mins | Ready in:

Ingredients

- 2lb   Pasta (any shape, I like to use radiatore)
- 1lg   Bottle of favorite Itailian dressing (I use Wishbone robust)
- 1   Cucumber (peeled and diced)

- 2   Scallions (chopped)
- 1jar   Black Olives (halved)
- 1jar   Green Olives (halved) with or without pimentos
- 1stick   Pepperoni (diced)
- 1block   Montergy Jack Cheese (cubed small)
- 1   Bell pepper (any color, red, yellow, or orange are sweeter)
- 1tsp   Dried Basil
- 1tsp   Dried Oregano
- 1tsp   Garlic Powder
- salt and pepper

Direction

- Cook pasta as instructed on box (al dente) remember to use plenty of salt in boiling water
- Drain and Rinse pasta in cold water
- Add pasta to large mixing bowl
- Add basil, oregano, garlic powder, salt, and pepper
- Mix well
- Next add all veggies, meat, and cheese
- Now add dressing (remember pasta will absorb dressing so reserve some to add right before serving
- Mix well, be sure everything get coated
- Put in refrigerator to chill (as least 45min to an hour)
- Enjoy!!!!

27. Emilys Macaroni Salad Recipe

Serving: 10 | Prep: | Cook: 10mins | Ready in:

Ingredients

- 1 lb elbow macaroni
- 1 bunch of celery, finely chopped
- 1 jar of polish pickle spears, finely chopped
- 1 cup mayonnaise
- 1/3 cup yellow deli mustard
- salt and pepper to taste

Direction

- Mix all ingredients in large bowl. Ta-da!
- P.S apples, cheese, and/or tuna can be added for additional flavor.

28. Firecracker Pasta Salad Recipe

Serving: 0 | Prep: | Cook: 18mins | Ready in:

Ingredients

- 13.5 oz Whole Wheat Rotini
- 1 cup yellow onion, diced
- 1 cup green bell pepper, diced
- 1 cup red bell pepper, diced
- 12 oz BBQ ham, beef or chicken, diced
- 1 1/2 cup ranch dressing
- 1 1/3 cup barbeque sauce
- 1/3 cup parmesan cheese, grated
- 1/4 cup scallions, minced
- Salt and pepper to taste
- My Meatless variation:
- 13.5 Whole Wheat Rotini
- 1 cup green pepper, diced
- 1 cup red pepper, diced
- 1 cup english cucumber, sliced crosswise then quatered
- 6 - 8 green onions siced with green parts
- 1 tbs mesquite liquid smoke
- 1 1/2 cup ranch dressing
- 1 1/2 cup honey barbeque sauce
- 1 1/2 cup shredded 5 cheese blend
- fresh ground pepper

Direction

- Cook the Rotini according to package directions. When pasta is "al dente", drain in colander
- Rinse pasta with cold water until cool to the touch. Drain well.
- Put pasta in large mixing bowl and add onions, pepper and meat (or cuke) and toss.
- Next mix in all remaining ingredients and blend well.

- Chill. Sprinkle with scallions (or more cheese) and serve.

29. Gazpacho Macaroni Salad Recipe

Serving: 6 | Prep: | Cook: 10mins | Ready in:

Ingredients

- 4 ounces uncooked macaroni
- 2-1/2 cups chopped, seeded tomatoes
- 1 cup finely chopped red onion
- 1 cup finely chopped cucumber
- 1/2 cup finely chopped celery
- 1/2 cup finely chopped green bell pepper
- 1/2 cup finely chopped red bell pepper
- 3 tablespoons cider vinegar
- 2 tablespoons finely chopped black olives
- 1 bay leaf
- 2 tablespoons minced fresh parsley
- 1 tablespoons fresh thyme
- 1 clove garlic, minced
- 3-4 dashes hot sauce
- fresh ground black pepper
- Garnish: whole olives, cucumber slices and dill sprigs.

Direction

- Cook pasta according to package directions, omitting salt in water.
- Drain and rinse well under cold water until pasta is cool.
- Drain well.
- Combine pasta and remaining ingredients in a bowl.
- Cover and refrigerate for 4 hours so flavors blend.
- Remove bay leaf before serving.
- Garnish with whole olives, cucumber slices and dill sprigs.
- Makes 6-1 cup servings.

30. Georges Grilled Chicken Macaroni Salad Recipe

Serving: 20 | Prep: | Cook: | Ready in:

Ingredients

- 6 LARGE GRILLED chicken breast fillets OR 10 SMALL (CUT INTO BITE SIZE PIECES)
- 3 BOXES OF elbow macaroni
- 1 PURPLE OR yellow onion(DICED FINELY)
- 1 BUNCH green onions (CHOPPED)
- 1 YELLOW OR red bell pepper(FINELY DICED)
- 1 green bell pepper FINELY DICED
- 5-6 LARGE eggs (BOILED) EACH EGG NEEDS TO BE CUT INTO FOURTHS OR YOU CAN DICE THE EGG INTO SMALLER PIECES
- 2 CUPS OF SHREDDED cheese (YOUR CHOICE) WE USE VELEVETTA
- 2 tomatoes (CHOPPED)
- 2 CUPS celery (FINELY CHOPPED)
- 1 JAR OF HELLMAN'S OR KRAFT MAYONAISE
- seasoning (I USE NATURES seasoning, YOU CAN USE TONY'S, SLAP YA MAMA, ETC.. YOUR CHOICE)
- parsley
- black pepper (TO TASTE)

Direction

- CHOP AND DICE ALL YOUR VEGETABLES
- GRILL THE CHICKEN BREAST
- BOIL THE ELBOW MACARONI
- COMBINE ALL INGREDIENTS TOGETHER
- SERVE
- REFRIGERATE LEFTOVERS

31. Grandmas Macaroni Salad Recipe

Serving: 8 | Prep: | Cook: 10mins | Ready in:

Ingredients

- 2 cups cooked macaroni (cook acording package directions & cool)
- 1 can red salmon or tuna (I like the hickory smoked tuna in this too)
- 1 bunch of celery, cut up
- 1 lg cucumber, diced
- 2 Tbs minced onion
- 2 plum tomatoes diced
- salt and pepper to taste
- salad dressing - like Miracle Whip - until it looks good... (I use Mayo most ot the time)

Direction

- Combine all ingredients and refrigerate until ready to serve.

32. Hawaiian Macaroni Salad Recipe

Serving: 10 | Prep: | Cook: 1hours15mins | Ready in:

Ingredients

- 1 Lb red potatoes
- 8 oz macaroni noodles
- 1 ½ cups chopped celery and mayo
- 1 cup shredded carrots
- 3 hard boiled eggs chopped
- ½ lb cooked ham cut into 1/3 inch cubes
- 1 cup frozen peas
- ½ cup red onion
- 1 tbsp Dijon mustard
- 1 tsp season salt & pepper

Direction

- 1. In 2 large pot boil macaroni and potatoes for 8 mins, drain well.
- 2. In a large bowl toss pasta and potatoes with remaining ingredients to combine.
- Refrigerate, covered, for about 1 hour so flavors can meld.

33. Hawaiian Macaroni Salad Recipe

Serving: 10 | Prep: | Cook: 10mins | Ready in:

Ingredients

- 1 bag macaroni noodles
- 1 1/2 c mayo
- 3/4 c milk
- 1/2 c teriyaki sauce (see my recipe if you want to make it yourself)
- 4 carrots ~ shredded
- 1 bunch green onion ~ chopped fine
- pepper

Direction

- Mix everything together, store in the fridge overnight
- Enjoy!

34. Hawaiian Style Macaroni Salad Recipe

Serving: 10 | Prep: | Cook: 15mins | Ready in:

Ingredients

- 1 box macaroni of your choice
- 6 boiled eggs
- 1 grated carrot
- __additional add-ins may include, to your taste....
- onions finely chopped

- olives chopped
- 1 can well drained tuna
- 1 cup FROZEN petite peas
- 1/2 cup finely chopped celery
- 1 or more cups salad size cooked shrimp
- Dressing
- 1 cup MAYONAISE or more
- 2 T water
- 1/2 tsp rice vinegar (for a little tang)
- salt and pepper to taste
- **if desired
- 1/2 tsp good curry powder
- 1/2 tsp paprika
- 2 T milk
- 1 T sugar

Direction

- Cook macaroni according to package
- Rinse well and chill if possible
- Have boiled eggs prepared ahead of time
- Chop eggs and add to macaroni
- Add grated carrot to macaroni and any additional add-ins you desire
- Chill while mixing dressing
- Mix all dressing ingredients together, adding more mayonnaise or water as needed MAYONAISE IS A MUST!!!
- Mix all together well, keep chilled and serve

35. Homemade Macaroni Salad Recipe

Serving: 68 | Prep: | Cook: | Ready in:

Ingredients

- 1 pkg Kraft Dinner
- 2 cups shredded cabbage
- 1/2 cup chopped green pepper
- 1/4 cup finely chopped green onions
- 3 hard cooked eggs
- 1 cup mayonnaise
- 1/2 cup sour cream

- 1Tbsp prepared mustard
- 1/2 tsp salt

Direction

- Prepare macaroni and cheese as directed on the package.
- Add remaining ingredients and mix lightly.
- Chill several hours or overnight.

36. Incalata Con Pasta Rapido Y Facile Recipe

Serving: 8 | Prep: | Cook: 20mins | Ready in:

Ingredients

- The salad:
- • 1 lb uncooked pasta. I usually use three color rotini but any short pasta type will do.
- • 2 – 3 cups frozen mixed veggies, to taste. I use the carrot, green bean, pea and corn mix.
- • 2 – 3 Tbs chopped ripe olives, to taste.
- • 2 – 4 sliced fresh mushrooms, depending on size.
- The dressing:
- • 1 cup real mayonnaise.
- • 1 tsp Dijon mustard, to taste.
- • 2 Tbs dry white wine or vinegar, to taste.
- • A pinch of sweet basil.
- • A sprig of cilantro, chopped.
- • 1 tsp chili powder, to taste.
- • Salt and fresh ground pepper to taste.

Direction

- 1. Cook the pasta just al dente, rinse with cold water and drain
- 2. Mix all of the Dressing ingredients together until smooth and creamy.
- 3. Mix all of the salad ingredients and the dressing in a large bowl and toss until well mixed.
- You can garnish this with a few sprigs of parsley or cilantro.

37. KFC Macaroni Salad Copycat Recipe

Serving: 6 | Prep: | Cook: 10mins | Ready in:

Ingredients

- 7 ounces Box elbow macaroni, cooked according to directions
- 2 Ribs celery minced fine
- 1 tablespoon Dry minced onion
- 1/3 cup Diced sweet pickles
- 1 1/2 cups Fat free Miracle Whip
- 1/2 cup Fat free mayo
- 1/4 teaspoon black pepper
- 1/4 teaspoon dry mustard
- 1 teaspoon sugar
- salt to taste

Direction

- Combine everything just as listed.
- Refrigerate salad tightly covered several hours before serving.

38. Kentucky Fried Chicken Secret Macaroni Salad Recipe

Serving: 8 | Prep: | Cook: 12mins | Ready in:

Ingredients

- 8 Oz of elbow macaroni
- 2 Ribs celery minced fine
- 1/4 cup thinly diced carrots (very thin!)
- 1 tablespoon Dry minced onion
- 1/3 cup Diced sweet pickles
- 1 1/2 cups Miracle Whip
- 1/2 cup Hellmans Mayonaise
- 1/4 teaspoon black pepper
- 1/4 teaspoon dry mustard

- 1 teaspoon sugar
- salt to taste

Direction

- Cook elbow macaroni to package directions, drain well and let cool.
- Combine remaining ingredients in a mixing bowl and mix well.
- Fold mixture into macaroni and toss to combine. Cover and let chill for several hours.

39. Leftover Macaroni And Pea Salad Recipe

Serving: 8 | Prep: | Cook: 120mins | Ready in:

Ingredients

- Here's what I had:
- 1/2 cup uncooked salad pasta or macaroni (I actually used 2 cups, because that was the serving size I broke my huge bag of macaroni into!!)
- 1 lb. can of sweet (English) peas (I used the rest, probably about 1 cup of my Publix brand grocery store frozen bag of peas!!)
- 1 small onion, chopped fine
- 2 slices american, cheddar or any favorite cheese, cut into small cubes (I used the rest of my Publix brand grocery store shredded cheddar cheese, maybe 1/2 to 1 cup, or so)
- salt and pepper, to taste
- Here's what I needed and had to buy:
- 2 stalks celery, chopped fine (only because I ran out!!) :(
- 1/4 cup Miracle Whip or mayonnaise (I used about 3/4 to 1 cup of mayo, due to the amount of pasta, also I use Duke's brand mayo, it's my favorite, much better than anything else I've tried!!) (also ran out of this....figures!!)
- Here's what I added into some of the left-over macaroni salad:
- 1/2 cup Durkee brand french fried onions
- 1/2 jalapeno pepper, chopped fine

- also, 1 dash or so of cayenne pepper

Direction

- Cook pasta according to package directions. Cool (maybe about 20 minutes or so, so the mayo won't get cooked.)
- Blend together the rest of the ingredients with cooled pasta.
- Cool again (that's what the 120 minutes is for. It will also be nice and chilled and the vegetables will be so crunchy!!!! Mmmmmmmmmm!!
- If you would like to add some meat, add some chopped cooked chicken or some cubed ham or even salami would be great..... Don't forget about pepperoni!!!
- If adding the Durkee onions, add at the very possible last minute you can get away with or they will get soggy!!
- Enjoy!!

40. MACARONI FRUIT SALAD Recipe

Serving: 8 | Prep: | Cook: 10mins | Ready in:

Ingredients

- 2 c. macaroni, uncooked (use elbow, shells or twists)
- 1 c. celery, sliced
- 1 lg. apple, diced & toss with lemon juice
- 1 c. seedless white grapes
- 1 (15 oz.) can pineapple chunks
- 1 (11 oz.) can mandarin orange segments, well drained
- 1 c. mini white marshmallows
- 1/2 c. mayonnaise or salad dressing
- 1/2 c. sour cream
- 1 tsp. sugar
- 1/8 tsp. nutmeg
- lettuce leaves
- .

Direction

- Cook macaroni, rinse and drain well.
- In large bowl, combine all ingredients except lettuce, mix well. Cover and chill thoroughly.
- When ready to serve you can place lettuce leaf on plate and fill with salad.

41. MACARONI AND CHEESE SALAD Recipe

Serving: 6 | Prep: | Cook: 10mins | Ready in:

Ingredients

- 1 package Kraft macaroni and cheese (prepare according to box)
- 1 medium tomato chopped
- Dash of pepper
- ¾ cup salad dressing
- ½ cup celery slices
- 1/3 cup chopped onion
- ½ teaspoon salt
- 3 hard boil eggs

Direction

- Mix all ingredients and chill. Add more salad dressing, if needed, before serving.

42. MACARONI SALAD Recipe

Serving: 5 | Prep: | Cook: 8mins | Ready in:

Ingredients

- Ingredients
- 2 cups uncooked elbow macaroni
- 4 hard-cooked egg, chopped fine
- 1 med onion, chopped fine
- 3 stalks celery, chopped
- 1 small red bell pepper, seeded and chopped
- 2 tablespoons dill pickle relish

- 2 cups creamy salad dressing (e.g. Miracle Whip)
- (I use 3/4 c Miracle Whip, the rest mayo)
- 3 tablespoons prepared yellow mustard
- 3/4 cup white sugar
- 2 1/4 teaspoons white vinegar
- 1/4 teaspoon salt
- 3/4 teaspoon celery seed

Direction

- Bring a pot of lightly salted water to a boil.
- Add macaroni, and cook for 8 to 10 minutes, until tender.
- Drain, and set aside to cool.
- In a large bowl, stir together the eggs, onion, celery, red pepper, and relish.
- In a blender, mix the salad dressing, mustard, white sugar, vinegar, salt and celery seed.
- Pour over the vegetables, and stir in macaroni until well blended.
- Cover and chill for at least 2 hour before serving.

43. Macaroni Chicken Salad Recipe

Serving: 12 | Prep: | Cook: 25mins | Ready in:

Ingredients

- 500g elbow macaroni, uncooked
- 2 pieces chicken breast
- 100g chopped celery
- 1 large carrot, chopped or shredded
- 2 tbsp pickle relish
- 1 apple, sliced into small cubes
- 4 pieces pineapple rings, sliced
- 1 big jar of mayonnaise
- 1/2 cup condensed milk
- 4 tbsp raisins
- 1 cup all purpose cream or heavy cream
- 2 cups grated cheese
- salt and ground black pepper to taste

Direction

- Boil water in a pot with a little salt and cooking oil. Put the elbow macaroni in boiling water and cook until it is firm to the bite (al dente). Drain.
- Boil the chicken breast in slightly salted water until tender. Drain and let it cool, then shred the chicken breast and discard the bones.
- In a large bowl, combine the cooked macaroni, shredded chicken, chopped celery, carrot, pickle relish, apples, pineapple slices and raisins. Season to taste with fine salt and ground black pepper.
- Add the mayonnaise, all-purpose cream and condensed milk. Lastly, add the cheese and mix well. Adjust the seasonings according to your taste.
- Refrigerate for a few hours to chill. Serve cold.

44. Macaroni Medley Salad Recipe

Serving: 10 | Prep: | Cook: 15mins | Ready in:

Ingredients

- 1 package (7 1/4 oz) macaroni and cheese
- 1/4 cup milk
- 1/2 cup butter or margarine
- 2 tablespoons Dijon mustard
- 4 hard cooked eggs, chopped
- 2 medium tomatoes, chopped
- 1 small cucumber, peeled and chopped
- 2 teaspoons chopped onion
- 1/2 teaspoon salt
- 1/8 teaspoon pepper

Direction

- Prepare macaroni and cheese with milk and butter according to package directions.
- Place macaroni in large bowl and cool for 15 minutes.
- Stir in mayonnaise, mustard.
- Fold in remaining ingredients. Keep cool until serving.

45. Macaroni Salad Recipe

Serving: 116 | Prep: | Cook: 10mins | Ready in:

Ingredients

- 2 cups drained cooked elbow macaroni (1 cup uncooked)
- 1 can chunk pineapple (drained)
- 6 apples peeled and chopped
- 1 can Mandarins (opt)
- Sauce:
- 4 eggs
- 2 cups icing sugar
- 1/2 cup lemon juice
- 1 pint whipping cream

Direction

- Combine Macaroni, pineapple, mandarins and apples set aside
- Cook eggs sugar and juice until thick Looks like lemon pie filling
- Fold into apple mixture after cooled, Keep cold
- Just before serving whip the cream and fold into the cold macaroni mixture

46. Macaroni Shrimp Salad Recipe

Serving: 4 | Prep: | Cook: 10mins | Ready in:

Ingredients

- 12 ounce package salad macaroni
- 1 pound salad size shrimp
- 1/4 cup mayonnaise
- 3 teaspoons prepared mustard
- 1 teaspoon chili powder
- 1 teaspoon pappy seasoning
- 1 large stock celery chopped
- 2 tablespoons white onion chopped
- 8 ounces canned sliced olives

- 1 teaspoon salt

Direction

- Cook macaroni according to directions then drain in colander and rinse with cold water.
- Mix mayonnaise and mustard together to taste then add remaining ingredients and mix well.
- Chill in refrigerator several hours before serving.
- Keep refrigerated until ready to eat.

47. Macaroni Supper Salad Recipe

Serving: 6 | Prep: | Cook: 10mins | Ready in:

Ingredients

- 1 8 oz. package small shell macaroni
- 2 cups diced cooked ham or ham luncheon meat
- 1/2 c. coarsely grated carrot
- 1/4 cup chopped onion
- 1/4 cup chopped green pepper
- 1 tsp salt
- 1 cup mayonaise
- 1 8 oz can tomato sauce

Direction

- Cook, drain and rinse macaroni according to package directions.
- Mix ham, carrots, onion, and green pepper and salt in large bowl.
- Blend Mayonnaise and tomato sauce
- Pour over salad ingredients: toss lightly to mix
- Chill thoroughly.
- Serve on crisp salad greens

48. Macaroni Tuna Salad Recipe

Serving: 4 | Prep: | Cook: 5mins | Ready in:

Ingredients

- 12 ounces canned water packed albacore tuna drained and flaked
- 8 ounce package small shell macaroni
- 2 hard boiled eggs finely chopped
- 1/4 cup green or red pepper chopped
- 2 stalks celery chopped
- 1 bunch green onions chopped
- 1 cup frozen green peas cooked and cooled
- 3/4 cup mayonnaise
- 2 tablespoons pickle relish
- 1 teaspoon salt
- 1 teaspoon freshly ground black pepper

Direction

- Cook macaroni according to package directions then drain and rinse with cold water. Allow to cool then add tuna, eggs, pepper, celery, onions and peas and mix well.
- In a small bowl mix together mayonnaise, pickle relish, salt and pepper.
- Add to the macaroni and mix well then place in refrigerator several hours before serving.

49. Macaroni And Shrimp Salad Recipe

Serving: 14 | Prep: | Cook: 10mins | Ready in:

Ingredients

- 16 oz. bag salad or elbow macaroni
- 1 cup celery, diced fine
- 1 cup green onions, chopped (include some of the green part)
- 1/2 cup green pepper, diced fine
- 1 lb. salad shrimp, cooked and shelled
- 1 cup mayonaise
- 5 Tbs. Dijon mustard
- 1 tsp. celery seed
- 1 tsp. horseradish
- 2 to 3 Tbs. sweet pickle juice from a jar of pickles

- salt and pepper to taste
- 5 hard boiled eggs

Direction

- Cook the pasta according to package directions. Rinse so that pasta is cool. Drain well.
- Place the celery, green onions and green pepper in a large bowl. Add the cooked and drained pasta. Stir to evenly incorporate celery, onions and pepper.
- Add the shrimp and mayonnaise and evenly stir in.
- Add the mustard, celery seed, horseradish, pickle juice and salt and pepper. Stir until all is well combined. Chill overnight.
- Peel and slice hard boiled eggs and place on top of salad before serving.

50. Mega Egga Macaroni Salad From Big Daddys House Recipe

Serving: 6 | Prep: | Cook: 12mins | Ready in:

Ingredients

- 2 pounds elbow noodles
- 12 hard boiled eggs, peeled and diced
- 1/2 onion, finely diced
- 4 celery stalks, finely diced
- 1/4 cup pickle relish (dill)
- 3 cups heavy mayonnaise (Kraft real mayo)
- 2 tablespoons salt
- 1 teaspoon coarsely cracked black pepper
- Dash hot sauce
- 1 tablespoon worcestershire sauce

Direction

- Directions
- In a large pot with salt, boil pasta for 12 to 15 minutes until cooked. Stir often.
- Drain and cool.
- Refrigerate for 30 minutes.

- In a large pot with a dash of salt, add eggs on medium high heat. Bring to a boil.
- Cover and remove from heat.
- Let eggs sit for 6 to 7 minutes.
- Remove eggs and shock in ice water.
- Once thoroughly cooled, peel eggs and roughly dice.
- Place pasta in a large bowl.
- Add onions, celery, eggs, relish, mayonnaise, salt and pepper, hot sauce and Worcestershire.
- Mix until well combined.

51. Mrs. B's Macaroni Salad By Jessie Recipe

Serving: 16 | Prep: | Cook: 45mins | Ready in:

Ingredients

- 1- 1 lb. box of salad macaroni (ditalini)
- salt, olive oil for prepping pasta
- 2 small tomatoes
- 3 stalks of celery
- 1/2 bell pepper - any color
- 3 green onions - chopped
- 1 teaspoon mustard
- 4 Tablespoons of mayonaise
- 1 dash of lemon pepper to taste
- 1/2 cup of cilantro(leaves only) diced

Direction

- Cook Macaroni according to box directions. A little olive oil in the water will keep pasta from sticking together.
- Dice celery, tomatoes, bell pepper, and green onion
- In a large bowl, add mayonnaise, mustard and combine. Add tomatoes, bell pepper, celery, green onions and cilantro.
- Add the macaroni and toss.
- Add Lemon Pepper and salt to taste.
- Refrigerate for about an hour.

52. My Macaroni Salad Recipe

Serving: 8 | Prep: | Cook: 10mins | Ready in:

Ingredients

- 8 ounces elbow macaroni
- 8 ounce package sharp cheddar cheese crumbles
- 1/2 cup mayonnaise
- 10 grape tomatoes
- 1/2 cup chopped sweet pickles
- salt to taste
- pepper to taste

Direction

- Cook macaroni according to package directions. Mine called for 10 minutes and that is the "cook time" shown.
- Drain macaroni and run cool water over it until it cools off. Set your colander over paper towels to drain while you prepare your other ingredients.
- Slice tomatoes lengthwise, then cut each half into 3 or 4 pieces.
- Chop pickles. Today I used the little tiny whole sweet pickles.
- Place drained macaroni in a large bowl and season with salt and pepper as desired.
- Add the mayonnaise and stir to coat the macaroni evenly.
- Add cheese and mix, then stir in pickles and tomatoes.
- Chill at least a couple hours, or overnight if possible.
- Stir before serving. Add additional mayonnaise if needed, or additional salt and pepper.

53. Never Fail Macaroni Salad Recipe

Serving: 12 | Prep: | Cook: 20mins | Ready in:

Ingredients

- 1 pound tri colored spriral pasta
- 5 hard boiled eggs
- 2 medium carrots shredded
- 1 large green pepper, diced
- 1 bunch green onions, chopped
- 3 stalks celery, chopped
- 1 envelope Good Season's Italian salad dressing mix
- 1 quart mayonnaise

Direction

- Cook pasta per package
- Boil eggs and cool
- Mix all ingredients in a large bowl
- Refrigerate 3 to 8 hours

54. Over The Top Macaroni Salad Recipe

Serving: 8 | Prep: | Cook: 30mins | Ready in:

Ingredients

- 5 ounces small Sea shell macaroni
- 1 almost ripe avocado, cut in ½" dice
- 4 slices bacon, fried crispy
- 2 ounces cheddar cheese, cut in ¼" chunks
- 2 hard boiled eggs, cut in ¼" chunks
- 2 roma tomatoes, seeded and cut in small chunks
- 2 Tbsp. sweet yellow onion, chopped fine
- 2 Tbsp. chopped Italian parsley
- ½ cup mayonnaise
- ¼ cup sour cream
- ¼ teas. celery salt
- pepper to taste

Direction

- Boil macaroni according to directions on package. Drain and rinse in cold water. Set aside.
- Combine bacon, cheese, eggs, tomatoes, onion and parsley. Add macaroni and stir to combine.
- Mix together mayonnaise and sour cream with celery salt and pepper. Add to salad and stir.
- Lastly add avocado and stir gently to combine. Refrigerate until ready to serve. Having avocado in this salad, it should be consumed the same day or the avocado discolors.
- Also, using an avocado that is almost ripe works best. If they are too ripe, it just goes to mush when you mix it in the salad.

---

55. Over The Top Macaroni Salad Recipe

Serving: 5 | Prep: | Cook: 45mins | Ready in:

Ingredients

- The Top macaroni Salad
- Ingredients :
- 5 ounces small Sea shell macaroni
- 1 almost ripe avocado, cut in ½" dice
- 4 slices bacon, fried crispy
- 2 ounces cheddar cheese, cut in ¼" chunks
- 2 hard boiled eggs, cut in ¼" chunks
- 2 roma tomatoes, seeded and cut in small chunks
- 2 Tbsp. sweet yellow onion, chopped fine
- 2 Tbsp. chopped Italian parsley
- ½ cup mayonnaise
- ¼ cup sour cream
- ¼ teas. celery salt
- pepper to taste
- --

Direction

- How to make it:
- Boil macaroni according to directions on package. Drain and rinse in cold water. Set aside.
- Combine bacon, cheese, eggs, tomatoes, onion and parsley. Add macaroni and stir to combine.
- Mix together mayonnaise and sour cream with celery salt and pepper. Add to salad and stir.
- Lastly add avocado and stir gently to combine. Refrigerate until ready to serve. Having avocado in this salad, it should be consumed the same day or the avocado discolors.
- Also, using an avocado that is almost ripe works best. If they are too ripe, it just goes to mush when you mix it in the salad.

---

56. PA Dutch Sweet Sour Macaroni Salad Recipe

Serving: 12 | Prep: | Cook: 10mins | Ready in:

Ingredients

- 1/2 pound mararoni, cooked until tender
- 1 cup mayo
- 1/4 cup yellow mustard
- 1 cup chopped celery
- 1 cup chopped onions
- 1/2 dozen hard boiled eggs
- 2 grated carrots

Direction

- Put in double boiler and boil: 1 1/2 cups sugar, 1/4 cup flour, 1 1/2 cup water, 1/2 cup vinegar.
- Add mayo and mustard to boiled mixture. Whisk until smooth.
- Pour this dressing over macaroni and other ingredients except eggs.
- Slice hard boiled eggs on top
- NOTE: this will start out very runny. It needs to sit several hours or overnight to thicken.

57. Pasta Veggie Salad Recipe

Serving: 12 | Prep: | Cook: 1hours | Ready in:

Ingredients

- 16 ounces small shell pasta, cooked,, drained and cooled
- 2 tablespoons vegetable or light olive oil
- 2 tablespoons cider vinegar
- 2 tablespoons honey
- 1 teaspoon dried dill weed
- Garlic powder to taste
- 1/2 large cucumbler, seeded and diced
- 2 to 3 large ripe tomatoes, seeded and diced
- 1/2 large green bell pepper, seeded and diced
- 1/2 cup carrot, shredded
- 1/2 cup sweet or red onion, diced
- Mayonnaise
- Salt and ground black pepper to taste

Direction

- Whisk together oil, vinegar, honey, dill weed, garlic powder, salt and pepper. Add to cooled pasta and toss to coat.
- Cover and chill 30 minutes.
- Add cucumber, tomato, green bell pepper, carrot and onion to pasta. Toss to combine.
- Add enough mayonnaise to moisten salad to taste. Cover and chill overnight.
- Add additional mayonnaise before serving if necessary.

58. Pennsylvania Dutch Macaroni Salad Recipe

Serving: 0 | Prep: | Cook: 30mins | Ready in:

Ingredients

- 1 lb. macaroni
- 2 carrots, cut fine
- 1 c. celery, cut fine
- 1 small onion, chopped fine, if desired
- 1 green or red pepper, cut fine
- 6 hard boiled eggs, cut up
- fresh parsley
- salt and pepper
- Pennsylvania Dutch salad dressing (recipe follows)

Direction

- Cook macaroni in salted water for 20 minutes. Add 1/2 teaspoon yellow food coloring while boiling macaroni. Cool in kettle by running cold water over macaroni. Drain in colander. Serve with following salad dressing.
- COOKED PENNSYLVANIA DUTCH SALAD DRESSING:
- 3 eggs
- 1 tbsp. flour
- 1 c. sugar
- 1/2 c. vinegar
- 1 c. water
- 1/2 t. celery seed
- Salt
- Combine above ingredients and cook. When thick, add 2 large tablespoons Miracle Whip or other salad dressing. Mix with macaroni for salad.

59. Pineapple Pasta Salad Recipe

Serving: 10 | Prep: | Cook: 40mins | Ready in:

Ingredients

- 1 Box shell pasta
- 1 Block cheddar cheese(Chopped Into tiny cubelike chunks)
- 3 bundles spring onions (Chopped)
- 2 Cans Dole pineapple slices(Drained & Cut into Chunks)
- Mayonaise 2-3 tbsp. use one at a time so not to be to wet or it wont be good consistency.
- dill weed(1 Tbsp)or more up to you.

- dill pickle relish(1 -2 tbsp)

Direction

- Boil your Shell Pasta until done not to soft, but done. Drain & Rinse Well with COLD water. Let Pasta drain very well. Set aside & chop up your green onions, cheese, and pineapple. Then put Pasta in Big Bowl add your mayo stir till mixed in. Then add in onions, pineapple, dill weed, dill pickle relish. Mix together until well incorporated. Then Add in your Cheese last because it tends to go to bottom, mix in & then cover & put into fridge to chill for at least 2 hours. It's really great if you make it a day ahead of time, and let sit in fridge overnight.
- I hope you enjoy this recipe! :)

60. Ranch Macaroni Salad Recipe

Serving: 8 | Prep: | Cook: 1hours |Ready in:

Ingredients

- 1 box mini penne, cooked according to package directions, I like mine el dente
- 1 small tomato, seeded and chopped
- 1-2 stalks celery, chopped
- 4-6 radishes, chopped
- 1/4 cup cucumber, chopped
- 2 scallions, chopped up to light green
- 1/2 small bell pepper, any color and chopped
- 1 8 oz. bottle ranch dressing
- salt and pepper to taste

Direction

- In large mixing bowl, combine all ingredients
- If I have any cooked bacon on hand I crumble it into the salad but that's not often around here....never any bacon leftover!!!

61. Ranch Noodle Salad Recipe

Serving: 8 | Prep: | Cook: 30mins |Ready in:

Ingredients

- pasta elbow noodles or your choice, ranch dressing pack of Hidden Valley Homemade packages.Or your choice of Ranch, peas, shredded carrots, bacon bits from jar or cooked & diced/chopped. Shredded cheddar cheese & white Mozzarella shredded cheese.

Direction

- In a pot boil pasta ever so gently until done don't overdo it, al dente. Put into a colander & run cool water over it, put aside. In a big mixing bowl add pasta & cooled steamed shredded carrots & peas. Toss gently. In another bowl mix Hidden Valley ranch dressing, mayo, milk & stir or shaker method in bottle jar, it is good to make this one a day ahead enhanced flavor blended. Add bacon bits to dressing. Then add this ranch dressing to the pasta/veggie mix. Stir & chill in frig. Ahead of dinner. To leave enough time for chilling.

62. Sadies Macaroni And Shrimp Salad Recipe

Serving: 6 | Prep: | Cook: 120mins |Ready in:

Ingredients

- 1-1/2 cups uncooked elbow macaroni
- 1 lb shrimp
- 1/2 cup chopped green onions
- 1/2 cup celery; sliced fine
- 1/2 cup sliced black pitted olives
- 1/4 cup dill pickles; chopped fine
- 1/2 teaspoon salt
- 1/2 teaspoon fine ground white pepper
- 6 hard boiled eggs; coarsely chopped

- 1 cup Sadie's Salad Dressing; * See Recipe

Direction

- Cook the eggs and refrigerate until needed.
- Cook, and peel the shrimp. Refrigerate until ready to mix.
- Cook macaroni, chill in iced water to cool, then drain.
- In a large bowl, mix macaroni, shrimp, onions, celery, olives, pickles, salt and pepper and toss well, then add chopped eggs and gently toss to mix.
- Spoon on the dressing and gently toss to mix thoroughly. Refrigerate until ready to serve.
- Note: Sadie is from Natchitoches, Louisiana, is pronounced [NAK-ah-dish]. I never met her but her salad is a real crowd pleaser.

63. Shrimp And Macaroni Salad Recipe

Serving: 8 | Prep: | Cook: 15mins | Ready in:

Ingredients

- 1 c. mayonaise (not Helman's)
- 1 tsp. seasoned salt
- 1 tsp. celery seed
- 1 tsp. salt
- 1/2 tsp. pepper
- 3 tblsp. spicy brown mustard
- 3 ribs celery, chopped
- sm. container grape tomatoes or halved cherry tomatoes
- small bunch of green onions, chopped
- 1 1/2 lbs. jumbo shrimp shelled and cooked
- 16 oz. shell macaroni (cooked in salted water)

Direction

- Combine mayo, seasonings, and mustard in a large bowl. Mix well. Add celery, tomatoes, and green onions. Mix well. Add the shrimp

and macaroni, and mix well. Refrigerate for about 2 hours before serving.

64. Shrimp Macaroni Salad Recipe

Serving: 1012 | Prep: | Cook: |Ready in:

Ingredients

- 2 1/2 cups of cooked shell macaroni
- 1 1/2 lb small cooked shrimp
- 2/3 cup chopped celery
- 1 medium chopped onion
- 1 cup mayo
- 3/4 cup catsup
- 1/2 cup sweet pickle relish
- 2-3 tabs. lemon juice
- 2 dashes hot sauce
- 1/2 teaspoon salt
- 1/4 teaspoon pepper

Direction

- Put first 4 ingredients in a large bowl
- Mix next 7 ingredients and Blend well, then pour over salad and stir. Ref until chilled.
- When I serve this, I sometimes put it in a large bowl with a center small bowl that I fill with cocktail sauce, and hang some whole shrimp off the sides of the small bowl. Put on a platter and put crackers around the bowl.

65. Shrimp And Macaroni Salad Recipe

Serving: 10 | Prep: | Cook: 10mins |Ready in:

Ingredients

- 1 lb. small shell macaroni, cooked al dente
- ½ lb. small fresh salad shrimp, rinsed and drained
- ½ cup chopped celery

- ½ cup chopped green pepper
- ½ cup chopped red onion
- 1 small jar pimento pieces
- 2 hard boiled eggs, chopped
- 3 Tbsp. chopped fresh dill
- 2 Tbsp. chopped fresh parsley
- 1 teas. season salt
- ½ teas. fresh ground pepper
- 1 cup mayonnaise
- 2 Tbsp. milk

Direction

- Put first eight ingredient is large salad bowl.
- In a small bowl mix together Season salt, pepper, mayonnaise and milk. Mix well and pour over salad ingredients. Stir to combine and cover with plastic wrap. Refrigerate for at least 4 hours for flavors to blend.

66. Southern Macaroni Salad Recipe

Serving: 4 | Prep: | Cook: | Ready in:

Ingredients

- 2 cups cooked macaroni, drained, rinsed, cooled
- 2 hard-cooked eggs, chopped
- 1/4 cup chopped celery
- 1/4 cup chopped onion
- 1/3 to 1/2 cup mayonnaise or salad dressing
- 2 teaspoons sugar
- 2 teaspoons vinegar
- 1/2 teaspoon salt, or to taste
- 1/2 teaspoon prepared mustard
- pepper, to taste

Direction

- Combine all macaroni salad recipe ingredients, using about 1/3 cup of mayonnaise and stir well.
- Add a little more mayonnaise, if necessary.
- Taste and adjust seasonings.

- Cover and chill for 2 hours before serving.

67. Spinach And Orzo Salad

Serving: 10 | Prep: | Cook: 10mins | Ready in:

Ingredients

- 1 (16 ounce) package uncooked orzo pasta
- 1 (10 ounce) package baby spinach leaves, finely chopped
- ½ pound crumbled feta cheese
- ½ red onion, finely chopped
- ¾ cup pine nuts
- ½ teaspoon dried basil
- ¼ teaspoon ground white pepper
- ½ cup olive oil
- ½ cup balsamic vinegar

Direction

- Bring a large pot of lightly salted water to a boil. Add orzo and cook for 8 to 10 minutes or until al dente; drain and rinse with cold water. Transfer to a large bowl and stir in spinach, feta, onion, pine nuts, basil and white pepper. Toss with olive oil and balsamic vinegar. Refrigerate and serve cold.
- Nutrition Facts
- Per Serving:
- 490.5 calories; protein 15.8g 32% DV; carbohydrates 49g 16% DV; fat 26.9g 41% DV; cholesterol 25mg 8% DV; sodium 349.2mg 14% DV.

68. Spiral Macaroni Salad Recipe

Serving: 6 | Prep: | Cook: 15mins | Ready in:

Ingredients

- 8 ounce package spiral macaroni
- 1 cup cherry tomatoes halved

- 1 cup shredded cheddar cheese
- 1 small cucumber peeled and cut into chunks
- 2 tablespoons chopped green pepper
- 2 tablespoons chopped celery
- 2 tablespoons chopped green onion
- 1 tablespoon pickle relish
- 1/4 cup mayonnaise
- 1/2 teaspoon prepared mustard
- 1 pinch dill seeds
- 1 pinch celery salt
- 1 pinch celery seeds

Direction

- Cook macaroni according to package directions then drain.
- Rinse macaroni with cold water then drain.
- Combine macaroni and next 7 ingredients then toss gently.
- Combine remaining ingredients and mix well then pour over salad and toss gently.
- Cover and chill at least 1 hour before serving.

69. Tarragon Macaroni Salad Recipe

Serving: 4 | Prep: | Cook: 10mins | Ready in:

Ingredients

- 1 cup sugar
- 1/4 cup flour
- 1/4 cup tarragon vinegar
- 1-1/2 cups water
- 1/4 cup mustard
- 1 cup celery chopped
- 1/2 cup carrots chopped
- 4 hard boiled eggs
- 1/2 pound cooked macaroni
- 1 teaspoon salt
- 1 teaspoon freshly ground black pepper
- 1 teaspoon celery seed
- 1/4 cup mayonnaise

Direction

- Cook sugar, flour, vinegar and water until thick then add mustard.
- In large bowl combine macaroni, carrots, celery and hard boiled eggs.
- Add cooked mixture and mayonnaise until desired consistency.
- Add salt, pepper and celery seed then chill and serve.

70. Tasty Tuna Macaroni Salad Recipe

Serving: 8 | Prep: | Cook: | Ready in:

Ingredients

- Tasty tuna macaroni Salad
- tuna has a tangy zip in this lively new twist on a favorite classic.
- 2 cups (7 oz.) elbow macaroni, cooked, drined
- 1 can (6 oz.) tuna, drained. flaked
- 1 cup sliced celery
- 3/4 cup Miracle Whip or Miracle Whip light Dressing
- 1/4 cup each chopped green pepper and sliced grean onions
- 2 Tbsp. chopped pimiento
- salt and black pepper
- lettuce

Direction

- Mix macaroni, tuna, celery, dressing, green pepper, onions and pimiento.
- Season to taste with salt and black pepper.
- Refrigerate.
- Serve on lettuce-lined plates.
- Makes 8 servings.

71. Tri Color Noodle Salad Recipe

Serving: 6 | Prep: | Cook: 30mins | Ready in:

Ingredients

- 1 bag of tri-color noodles
- 1 cup of mayonnaise
- 2 green onions chopped into small pieces
- 1 can of tuna (drained)
- salt
- pepper

Direction

- Boil the noodles until tender in a hot pot of salted water
- Let cool
- Add the rest of ingredients and mix well
- Enjoy...

72. Tuna Macaroni Salad Recipe

Serving: 1214 | Prep: | Cook: 11mins | Ready in:

Ingredients

- 1 lb. small shells
- mayonnaise to taste; at least 3 cups
- 1 lg can of light-meat tuna packed in water; drained well
- 4 hard- boiled eggs, cooled and chopped
- 1 tsp. yellow mustard
- 5 stalks celery minced and squeezed through a napkin or cheesecloth
- 1 large carrot shredded and squeezed through a napkin or cheesecloth
- 2 tbs fresh parsley chopped
- sea salt
- Course ground pepper; lots of it.
- Depending on the Party suggestions:
- peas
- shrimp
- red onion

Direction

- Cook macaroni according to box directions. Drain and cool
- Combine all of the ingredients
- Refrigerate and taste before serving to see if needs more mayo, salt or pepper

73. Unique Macaroni Salad Recipe

Serving: 25 | Prep: | Cook: 30mins | Ready in:

Ingredients

- 1 pound shell macaroni cooked and drained well
- 2 cans pineapple tidbits (drained)
- 1 pounds ham - diced
- 1 large can peas, drained
- 1 large onion chopped FINE
- 4 cups celery -choppped FINE
- 1 dozen hard boiled eggs-peeled and chopped
- 1 small can/jar pimentos-chopped fine
- 5 oz cashew nuts
- Dressing:
- 1 qt. salad dressing (Miracle Whip)
- 3 tsp. light mustard
- 3 tsp. sugar
- salt to taste

Direction

- Combine all ingredients.
- Then add dressing.
- Stir gently.

74. Veggie And Macaroni Salad Recipe

Serving: 0 | Prep: | Cook: 45mins | Ready in:

Ingredients

- ingredients:
- 1 bottle of bernsteins resturant recipie Italian dressing.
- 1 sm box of whole wheat elbow macaroni or bowtie noodles.
- 1 -2 cups of grated finely carrots. i buy a bag of grated carrots
- 1 med. can of sliced olives.
- 2 lg. chopped tomatoes.
- 2 bunches of green onions chopped.
- 2 -2 1/2 cups of partially cooked broccoli
- 1- 1/2 to 2 cups of cooked peas. dont over cook

Direction

- (1) Boil macaroni till done. Then run under cold running water till cool.
- While macaroni is cooking (2) chop veggies and add to big mixing bowl.
- (3) When macaroni is cooled under running water at to mixing bowl with the veggies.
- (4) Pour 1 bottle of Bernstein's restaurant recipe Italian dressing over salad and mix well. (5) Chill for about an hour it's great to make ahead of time even for a day or evening ahead of time.

75. Windys Tuna Macaroni Salad Recipe

Serving: 8 | Prep: | Cook: 10mins |Ready in:

Ingredients

- 2 cups uncooked macaroni
- 4 hard-boiled eggs, chopped
- 1 (12-oz) can tuna, well drained
- 1 medium onion, chopped
- 2 stalks celery, chopped
- 1 small can sliced black olives, drain and discard liquid
- 1-1/2 cups Miracle Whip
- salt, to taste
- black pepper, to taste

Direction

- Cook macaroni per package directions. Drain well in a colander (do NOT rinse) and spread out on a jelly roll pan to cool.
- In a large mixing bowl, combine boiled eggs, tuna, onion, celery, black olives, salad dressing, salt and pepper. Fold in macaroni, mixing well.
- Cover and refrigerate for several hours to blend flavors.
- Serve well chilled.

Index

Conclusion

Thank you again for downloading this book!

I hope you enjoyed reading about my book!

If you enjoyed this book, please take the time to share your thoughts and post a review on Amazon. It'd be greatly appreciated!

Write me an honest review about the book – I truly value your opinion and thoughts and I will incorporate them into my next book, which is already underway.

Thank you!

If you have any questions, **feel free to contact at:** *author@ciderrecipes.com*

Elise Tobin

ciderrecipes.com

Made in United States
Cleveland, OH
06 July 2025

18279753R00020